# Britain since 1930

Barry Holley

TLEPOOL BOROUG
THDRAWN
LIBRARIES

Linked to the Local Community during the Second World War

Oxfo D0319444 4

The publishers wish to thank the following for permission
to reproduce copyright material:

Front cover: reproduced by permission of Royal Mail; p.1 Trustees of the Imperial War
Museum, London; p.4 *top* Hillingdon Borough Libraries, *bottom* North Yorkshire County
Library; p.5 *top left* Trustees of the Geffrye Museum, *top right* © Walt Disney, *bottom*
Imperial Publishing; pp.6 & 7 Cleveland County Archives; p.8 *top* Mansell Collection, *left
and bottom* The Hulton Deutsch Collection; p.9 *top* The Hulton Deutsch Collection,
*centre right* Daily Express; pp.10 & 12 The Hulton Deutsch Collection; p.13 *top* Punch,
*bottom* Trustees of the Imperial War Museum, London; p.15 *top* Popperfoto, *bottom* The
Hulton Deutsch Collection; p.16 *left* The Hulton Deutsch Collection, *right* Trustees of the
Imperial War Museum, London; p.17 *top and centre left* The Hulton Deutsch Collection,
*right* Süddeutscher Verlag Bilderdienst, *bottom* Topham Picture Source; p.18 Battle of
Britain Prints International; p.19 *top* D. C. Thomson & Co. Ltd. *bottom left* Mark
Bickerdike, *right* Trustees of the Imperial War Museum, London; p.20 Trustees of the
Imperial War Museum, London; p.21 *left* The Hulton Deutsch Collection, *right* Trustees
of the Imperial War Museum, London; p.22 *top* John Brennan, *bottom* Trustees of the
Imperial War Museum, London; p.23 Trustees of the Imperial War Museum, London;
p.24 The Hulton Deutsch Collection; p.25 David Low 'Evening Standard' 3/12/1942,
Centre for the Study of Cartoons, University of Kent; p.26 *top* Illustrated London News
Picture Library, *bottom left* Quadrant/Flight, *bottom right* Popperfoto; P.27 *top right and
bottom left* The Hulton Deutsch Collection, *centre* BBC Photo Library; p.28 The Hulton
Deutsch Collection; p.29 *top and centre* Andes Press Agency/Carlos Reyes, *bottom* Sally
and Richard Greenhill; p.30 York Castle Museum; p.31 Topham Picture Source, *inset*
Manchester Museum of Science and Industry; p.32 Topham Picture Source; p.33 *top*
ZEFA, *right* Daily Express; p.34 *top right* Topham Picture Source, *left* Rex Features; p.35
*top* Topham Picture Source, *right* DHL, *bottom* Rex Features; p.36 National Motor
Museum, Beaulieu; p.37 *top and centre* Milepost, *bottom* Topham Picture Source; p.38
Bridgeman Art Library/Illustrated London News; p.39 *top* The Hulton Deutsch
Collection, *centre* British Motor Industry Heritage Trust/Rover Group, *bottom* Wellcome;
p.40 Ronald W. Weir Photography; p.41 © Mo Wilson; p.42 Alpha Photographic Press
Agency; p.43 *top* Rex Features, *bottom* Q.A. Photo Library; p.44 *top* Topham Picture
Source, *bottom* Rex Features; p.45 *top* Tony Stone Images, *bottom* Still Pictures/C & C
Heldur Netocny; p.47 Eden Camp; back cover Topham Picture Source.

Illustrations by: Victor Ambrus, John Brennan, John Davis, Lovell Johns,
Bernard Long, Chris Molan, Tony Morris and Graham Smith.

Oxford University Press, Walton Street, Oxford OX2 6DP

*Oxford   New York   Toronto*
*Delhi   Bombay   Calcutta   Madras   Karachi*
*Kuala Lumpur   Singapore   Hong Kong   Tokyo*
*Nairobi   Dar es Salaam   Cape Town*
*Melbourne   Auckland   Madrid*

and associated companies in
*Berlin* and *Ibadan*

*Oxford* is a trade mark of Oxford University Press

© Oxford University Press, 1994

ISBN 0 19 917227 7

Typeset and designed by Positif Press, Oxford
Printed in Hong Kong

# Contents

# Home life

In the 1930s many new houses were built. These were mainly semi-detached with a garden. They were often built on the edges (or suburbs) of towns and cities.

However, many people still lived in older terraced houses. Some had no indoor toilet or bathroom. These rows of houses, all joined together, might have a back yard or a small garden. Some were 'back to back': joined to each other on both sides and also at the back.

In the 1930s there were thirty-nine adults and thirteen children living in thirteen of the houses shown in the photograph below. Each family had two rooms.

THE DAVIS ESTATE, WEST END ROAD, **SOUTH RUISLIP.**

Type R.P.41.   Three Bedrooms - Large Living Room - Combined Kitchen-Dining Room.

INTERIOR DECORATIONS TO PURCHASER'S CHOICE.

NO ROAD CHARGES, LEGAL COSTS OR SURVEY FEES.

TERRACED from **£565** FREEHOLD from **14/7** Weekly.

With 10 per cent. deposit, repayments are reduced to 12/6 Weekly.

LOW DEPOSIT from £30.

SEMI-DETACHED from **£615** FREEHOLD from **15/10** Weekly.

With 10 per cent deposit, repayments are reduced to 14/7 Weekly.

ACCOMMODATION.

*A 1930s advertisement for new homes near London.*

All the families shared the two taps and six toilets in the yard. There were no sinks for washing, and no pantries to store food. There was a tin bath. Water was heated in big kettles and pans over a coal fire.

How might these conditions affect the health of those living there?

What would it be like living here in winter?

*Alexandra Yard, York, in the early 1930s.*

By 1939 many homes had electricity. Electricity was soon used for lighting in place of gas lamps.

In what other ways has electricity changed people's lives?

What other *main* changes have taken place in homes and housing over the last sixty years?

For entertainment outside the home, people visited the local swimming baths, watched football matches or went to the 'pictures'. Every town had at least one picture house (cinema). Some films made in the 1930s are still shown today. For example, have you seen Walt Disney's film *Snow White and the Seven Dwarfs*?

© Disney

Entertainment in the home included reading. Families also listened to the gramophone and the wireless (radio). Popular programmes were *Children's Hour*, comedy shows, dance-band music and the BBC news.

Do you know why:

1. people called the radio a 'wireless'?
2. reading was a popular activity?

Collecting was a favourite hobby. Children collected and swapped such things as bus tickets, matchbox labels, cigarette cards and stamps. They also went train spotting.

*Cigarette cards came in sets such as famous film stars or cricketers. Here is Jack Hobbs, the famous English batsman.*

J. B. HOBBS (SURREY)

### CLASS ACTIVITY

What types of houses can you see near your school: detached, semi-detached, terraced, blocks of flats?

A local newspaper, or leaflets from estate agents, may help you to identify, to classify and to date the different kinds of houses.

Make a record of your survey, using material you have collected, maps and photographs.

Seeing differences
within the past and
between then and now.

# At school

In 1938 a new primary school was opened in a northern town. A Victorian school was pulled down to make way for it.

The photographs on this page show the old school before it was demolished.

Look carefully at the photographs of classrooms. Look at the furniture, the walls and windows, and the children.

What differences can you see between these classrooms?

From the outside

Old school – infants' classroom

Old school – junior classrooms

The photographs on this page show the new school in 1938.

From the outside

New school – infants' classroom

New school – junior classroom

In what ways are the old and new schoolrooms different from the classroom you are working in today?

Why do you think the changes have taken place?

Have any things stayed the same?

Which of the classrooms would you like to work in, and why?

In what ways do the schoolroom scenes provide evidence of how children learned in school in the 1930s?

## CLASS ACTIVITY

Ask older members of your family (parents, grandparents, aunts, uncles) about their schooldays. They may tell you about the way they were taught, the books they used, discipline, punishments, playground games, teachers and so on. Write down other things you may want to ask them about.

Perhaps you can borrow photographs, and photocopy them for a classroom display or to illustrate your findings.

Your own school may have artefacts (objects), and written or photographic records which can be used for a project or study of schooling in the past.

# *Hard times*

In the 1930s many people had no work. Others feared they might lose their jobs. Those who had no job (the unemployed) received unemployment payment from the state (the 'dole'). This was means tested, that is, the amount received depended on what income a family had. For example, a married man with a wife and two children might get 27 shillings (£1-36p) a week. However, if his wife had a job, then the dole was reduced by the amount she earned.

**What do you think is happening in this picture?**

People had less to spend. This affected shops and businesses. Many had to close down, so even more people were without work. Fewer goods were made. This is said to be a **depression**.

Which of these pairs of terms describes a depression?

| high unemployment few goods made | low unemployment few goods made |
|---|---|
| high unemployment many goods made | low unemployment many goods made |

The Depression of the 1930s was worst where one large industry employed many people. In Jarrow in north-east England, two-thirds of workers had no job when the ship-building yard closed.

Unemployment was high in northern England, Scotland and Wales. In south-east England, fewer people were out of work.

*Number of people unemployed each year:*

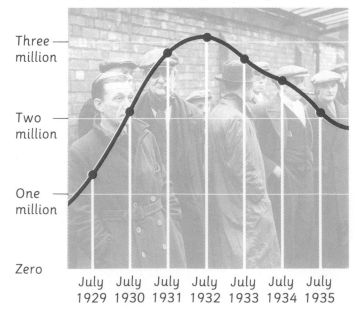

Three million

Two million

One million

Zero

July 1929　July 1930　July 1931　July 1932　July 1933　July 1934　July 1935

Look at this photograph and the cartoon below. Are there any similarities?

Do you think the cartoonist had seen the photograph? Say why you think this.

What is the man in the cartoon looking at?

One event which provided work and helped end The Depression is shown in the cartoon. What was it?

The pictures below show what some people ate each day. Do you think this was the daily diet of a very rich family, or of an ordinary family? Say why you think this.

Breakfast                    Midday meal                    Evening meal

What are the differences between this diet and the food you ate yesterday?

In the 1930s you might be able to buy a house for about £300 and a car for £100. Fish and chips cost one shilling (5p).

Look in the local newspapers. Find out the average price of a semi-detached house today, and the cost of the smallest new car. How much does a portion of fish and chips cost? How many times have these prices multiplied since the 1930s?

CLASS ACTIVITY

The coins we use today and the way we count our money have changed since the 1930s. Arrange a classroom display of 'old' and 'new' money. (You may use pictures, photocopies or rubbings instead of actual money.)

What are the differences in their value, shape, size, patterns and colour? In what units are old and new money counted?

# The road to war

Adolf Hitler was the leader of the Nazi Party in Germany. In 1933 he became the German Chancellor (Prime Minister).

He said he would:

1. get back the land Germany had lost as a result of the First World War
2. make the Jews less powerful in Germany
3. reduce unemployment by helping industry.

1. Jews and those people who did not agree with the ideas of the Nazis were put in large prison camps called concentration camps.

2. Hitler increased the size of the German army, navy and air force.

3. Hitler began to take over some of the countries next to Germany's borders. In 1936 he took over the Rhineland. In 1938 he took over Austria and the Sudetenland (part of Czechoslovakia

4. In September 1938 the British Prime Minister Neville Chamberlain met Hitler in Munich in Germany. He agreed that Hitler could keep the Sudetenland. The Czech people felt betrayed. But Chamberlain thought that he could prevent war by agreeing to Hitler's demands.

6. Hitler made an agreement with Joseph Stalin, leader of the Soviet Union. They planned to invade Poland. On 1 September 1939 the invasion began.

5. In March 1939 Hitler took the rest of Czechoslovakia. Britain and France now knew that appeasement (that is, giving in to Hitler) would not work. They got ready for war.

7. Britain demanded that Germany should withdraw from Poland. Hitler ignored the warning. On 3 September Britain and France declared war on Germany.

Make a time line of the main events which led to the outbreak of war in 1939.

Which of the events do you think were the most important causes of the war, and which were the least important?

Do you think the outbreak of war could have been avoided by taking different action, or not? Why do you think this is?

# Evacuation in 1939

The Government made plans to evacuate (move out) people from the cities and ports that would be targets for German air raids, if war broke out. So on Friday 1 September 1939 the evacuation began.

Children, pregnant women, the blind and the disabled were sent to live in the countryside.

Often whole schools were evacuated with their teachers.

> Children enjoy a little excitement, and they're much more adaptable than you think. They will be with the teachers and playmates they are used to, so their surroundings will not be entirely strange… You have done a brave and sacrificing thing in sending your children away from the danger areas. They are the future generation. The new Britain. When all this madness is over… it is our children who will have the task of building the world again.
>
> *Daily Mirror*, 4 September 1939

Who is the *Daily Mirror* telling about the benefits of evacuation?

What do you think of its advice?

Here each child is carrying a small oblong box. What was inside?

1. Food for the journey?

2. A gas mask to protect against poison gas?

3. School books?

"You're lucky to be able to have soap in your eye. In Germany the poor little boys can't have soap at all!"

Cartoons are drawn in order to appeal to newspaper readers.

Who was expected to laugh at this one: the boy or the family who had taken him in?

This letter is from a Liverpool girl:

Dear Mum,

I hope you are well. I don't like the man's face. I don't like the lady's face much. Perhaps it will look better in daylight. I like the dog's face best.

This is from a Yorkshire villager writing to *The Field* magazine, February 1940:

If air raids are coming many country people would prefer bombs to the evacuees they have got.

Why were mothers asked to send their children out of London?

Why might some mothers not want to send their children away?

MOTHERS
Send them out of London

Give them a chance of greater safety and health

CLASS ACTIVITY

Look at the pictures and written sources. Talk about what the evacuees might have taken with them.

What things would you take if you were evacuated today?

What does the evidence tell us about the feelings of the children and the people in the places they moved to?

Are any children being evacuated from their homes in the world today?

# The call to arms

When war was declared fit men of twenty and over had to be ready to join the armed forces.

Some countries fought on Britain's side. These included Jamaica, India, New Zealand and Australia.

People in important jobs like coal-mining did not have to 'join up'.

Why do you think this was so?

**The Air Force**

For his army to invade England successfully, Hitler needed control of the skies. In 1940 he sent the German air force (the **Luftwaffe**) to attack the **Royal Air Force** bases. The RAF pilots in their Spitfires and Hurricanes fought for several weeks, finally winning the **Battle of Britain**. After this Hitler put off his invasion plans.

*An RAF fighter pilot.*

I was a radio telephonist with direct communication with the pilots as they flew on their sorties against the Germans. And we used to see them out and then count them back, and then you'd wait, and there'd be some missing...

Why do you think people risked their lives as fighter pilots in the Battle of Britain?

**The Navy**

The **Royal Navy** tried to defend British colonies and her allies against invasion by Germany and her allies, Italy and Japan. An important task was to protect the convoys of ships bringing food and other supplies from America. German submarines – called **U-boats** – attacked with torpedoes.

After 1940 the RAF turned to bombing raids on German cities, arms factories and airfields.

*A U-boat in the Atlantic.*

14

## The Army

In 1941 Germany invaded Russia. Russia changed sides and joined Britain, the British Commonwealth, France and China. The United States of America also entered the war on the side of the Allies, after the Japanese attacked Pearl Harbor in 1941.

British soldiers and their allies fought long and difficult campaigns in the Far East and North Africa.

What made this a 'World' rather than a European War?

On 6 June 1944 (**D Day**) British, American and Canadian forces landed on the coast of Normandy in northern France (below). After long fierce fighting they began to drive the Germans out of France.

By May 1945 the advance of the Allies from the west and the Russians from the east had defeated Hitler and Germany.

The War in the Pacific ended in August 1945 when the United States dropped atomic bombs on the Japanese cities of Hiroshima and Nagasaki. Two hundred thousand people were killed and the cities destroyed.

What do you think of this action?

*Hiroshima after the atomic bomb was dropped.*

CLASS ACTIVITY

For a wall display make a time line of the main events of the Second World War. Add information from your class or school library.

# The Blitz

Look at the photographs of the Anderson and Morrison shelters on these two pages and describe how each was constructed.

What were the advantages and disadvantages of each type of shelter?

The German bombs dropped on towns killed and injured many thousands of people. Houses and important public buildings were damaged or destroyed.

British and American aircraft also dropped bombs on German towns.

Shelters were built to protect people from the bombs dropped during German air raids. Public shelters were made of concrete. In London, many people slept on the platforms of the Underground stations. Why was this?

Families put up their own shelters. Anderson shelters were built in people's gardens. Morrison shelters were used inside the house.

A Morrison shelter constructed in a living room.

Windows and car headlights had to be covered (blacked out) after dark. This was to make it difficult for German pilots to find towns at night. With no street lights, walking around was not easy.

What difficulties might the black-out rules cause for people?

Voluntary groups such as the Home Guard and the air raid wardens made sure that the black-out rules and air raid precautions were obeyed. They 'kept watch' against possible invasion.

16

When the air raid alarm was sounded many families took cover in an Anderson shelter like this in their garden.

Look carefully at the pictures of London and Dresden below.

What do the two scenes have in common?

What has caused the damage in both cities?

Give one short-term and one long-term result of bombing raids.

St Paul's Cathedral, London, after bombing raids in 1940.

Dresden after the Allied bombings in 1945.

The Prime Minister, Winston Churchill, made speeches which kept people's spirits up:

> We shall defend our island, whatever the cost may be... we shall fight in the fields and in the streets... we shall never surrender.

'Britain can take it' was the popular slogan.

Say why such speeches might help people to put up with air raids and other hardships.

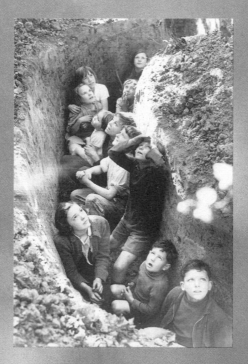

Children in Kent taking refuge in a trench during a German air raid.

CLASS ACTIVITY

Invite visitors who lived through an air raid into your school.

Prepare a list of questions that you want to ask them. Group the questions into topics.

You may be able to record the visit on video or audio tape.

*The Second World War affected people's lives in many different ways.*

# Helping the war effort

It wasn't just people in the armed forces who were affected by the War. Air raids and the absence of many men and women from home affected everyone. People also had to make changes in the way they lived from day to day.

What happened in your local area?

The next three sections will help you to carry out a class study of this topic.

For this section work in small groups. Choose one of the subjects in the boxes and find out all you can about it using the questions as a starting point.

Remember that talking to local people is very useful. You may be able to tape record or video interviews.

Look out for evidence around you: war memorials in the street and in churches.

Books, photographs, maps and newspapers can also tell you a lot. Try to collect artefacts like gas masks, helmets, old ration books, coins or medals. Try drawing some of them.

**Collecting salvage** Saving waste paper, jam jars, cardboard and scrap metal to make weapons was very important. Everyone felt they were helping with the war effort. Did your area play its part? What salvage collections are there today which are similar? Why?

**Entertainment** How did people keep themselves amused in shelters or at home? Who were the stars of radio and films? Were there dances, football matches or picnics? What toys and comics were popular?

**Our school** Was it here in 1939? If not, where was the local school? Did it stay open or were all the children evacuated (see pages 12-13)? Did it receive any evacuees?

**The streets** How have the shops and houses changed? Were any damaged by bombs? Look for photographs in newspapers and local history books from the library. Choose one and take a modern photo from the same spot and compare it then and now as in the pictures here.

D. C. Thomson & Co. Ltd 1993

The Dandy and The Beano first appeared in the 1930s. Here is Desperate Dan helping the war effort.

The photographs below show Cliff Side Gardens, Leeds, after a raid in 1941 and as it is today.

Perhaps you and your teacher can suggest other topics.

Was there an airfield or a prison camp nearby? Did American troops come to your area in the war? Where were the air raid shelters? Did local people have a big Victory party? What are the most lasting memories?

Some information you gather will have a national or international importance. For example, some people may tell you about their war service overseas. In fact for many it was the first time that they had travelled abroad.

Find the places they visited in an atlas and place these on a wall map, showing how far from home local people went in the War.

When you have finished, decide with your teacher the best way to display your findings.

By collecting this evidence you may be helping to preserve valuable information for historians in the future to find out more about this very important time.

A war-time poster asking people to repair their old clothes.

19

# Women at war

**For a healthy, happy job**

**Join the WOMEN'S LAND ARMY**

For details:  CLIVE UPTON
APPLY TO NEAREST W.L.A. COUNTY OFFICE OR TO W.L.A. HEADQUARTERS 6 CHESHAM PLACE LONDON S.W.1 STREET
Issued by the Ministry of Agriculture and the Ministry of Labour and National Service

This appeared in *The Farmers' Weekly* magazine, 3 December 1940:

'In Kent over 200 (land girls) worked… in danger… The tractors were so noisy that the drivers could not tell when the battle was overhead. So… they found themselves working with shrapnel falling all round them and even on their tractors. Not one of these girls asked for a transfer [a move]. Instead they applied [asked] for steel helmets – and got them!'

1. Give two reasons why women were needed to farm the land during the War.

2. Can you suggest why it was called the Women's Land Army?

3. In what ways does the poster try to make the job look attractive, and why?

The Women's Land Army reached its peak in 1943, at 87,000. Then more women were needed for aircraft and munitions factories.

Women played an important part in the war effort. They worked on the land and in factories, often taking on heavy jobs they were not used to so that the men could go and fight. Women drove buses and ambulances.

This is a wartime song about a factory girl:

It's the girl that makes the thing
    that drills the hole that holds the spring
That works the thingumabob
    that makes the engine roar.

And it's the girl that makes the thing
    that holds the oil that oils the ring
That works the thingumabob
    that's going to win the war.

Many women joined the women's branches of the armed forces such as the WAAF (Women's Auxiliary Air Force).

The wife of a schoolteacher in a Yorkshire village:

'Before the War local girls were very keen to work as domestic servants. Afterwards they were not interested; in any case, most of us could not afford the wages housemaids expected.'

Why do you think girls became less interested in work as domestic servants after the War?

CLASS ACTIVITY
Find out whether, in your local area, there:
1. was a munitions factory
2. were any brave deeds done by women
3. are any women who served in the WAAFs or the ATs
4. are any women who helped farm the land.

Record interviews with women from your area who can tell you about their work in the War.

Ask them to sum up the importance of going out to work for women generally.

Discuss how and why their memories and feelings differ.

# Rationing and recipes

The German navy attacked and sank ships bringing food to Britain. This meant that there was not enough of some kinds of food. From January 1940 food was rationed to try to make sure that everyone had their fair share. Everyone had a ration book. They used the coupons in the book to buy things like meat, butter, sugar and sweets.

Can you say how rationing might cause people to have a **healthier** diet?

By 1943 there were no bananas, ice cream, white bread or lemons to buy. However, people who were willing to pay high prices could buy most foods on the black market. It was difficult to get fresh eggs so dried or powdered eggs were used instead.

How might a shortage of some foods, eggs for example, cause people to invent new recipes and change their ways of cooking?

Some people tried to produce their own food. They grew vegetables and fruit. They kept bees and hens. Sometimes neighbours might keep a pig between them.

The government told people about ways to save food. For example, you might have less sugar in your tea, or drink one less cup a day.

Food was not the only thing in short supply. Other shortages included petrol, rubber and clothes.

Look at the cartoon characters of Potato Pete and Dr Carrot. Can you say why such vegetables were plentiful during the War? Say how showing such vegetables as 'characters' might encourage people to grow them and eat them?

I make a good Soup!

Says 'POTATO PETE'

22

DOCTOR CARROT the Children's best friend

VIT-A

DIG FOR VICTORY

### The Eggless Cake

**Ingredients: 1lb flour, 3oz sugar, 4oz raisins, 4oz margarine, a little mixed spice or ginger, teaspoon of bicarbonate of soda, ½ pint milk, teaspoon of vinegar.**

Cream the margarine and sugar. Dissolve the bicarbonate of soda in the milk, and add this alternately with the flour and fruit to the creamed margarine, beating all the time. Leave the mixture for approximately one hour to rise. Then add the vinegar, and bake in a lined and covered tin for 1½ hours in a moderate oven: Gas mark 4 (350°F).

What is the message of the poster?

What is the 'link' between the poster's message and Potato Pete and Dr Carrot?

Say how digging might help Britain to win the War.

Give two **causes** and two **results** of food shortages.

CLASS ACTIVITY

Look at the recipe for <u>The Eggless Cake</u>.

Could your class bake it in school? Or can you cook it at home and bring it into school?

Ask some people who remember rationing during the War to visit your class. Before they come, write down a list of questions or topics that you want to ask them about.

They might like to try a piece of your eggless cake (with a cup of sugarless tea!). They may tell you about the recipes they tried during the War.

Try to record the visit on an audio or video cassette.

# The coming of the Welfare State

When the War came to an end in 1945, everyone wanted a fresh start.

During the War some politicians had begun plans to make Britain a better place to live.

In 1942 William Beveridge wrote a report, suggesting that the State should look after everyone in need. Many people liked this idea of a **Welfare State**.

In 1945 the Labour Party won the General Election. The prime minister was Clement Atlee. The new government began to set up the Welfare State with the aim of looking after everyone 'from the cradle to the grave'. What do these words mean?

## Education

The 1944 **Education Act** had already provided free primary education for children up to eleven and secondary education for pupils over that age.

At eleven years of age pupils took the 11-plus examination. Those who passed could attend grammar schools. Others attended secondary modern schools. At the age of thirteen some children might have the chance of a practical education at a technical school.

School dinners, free school milk, medical inspection of pupils and special schools for handicapped children, were also part of the Act.

## Workers' rights

In 1946 it became law that full-time workers and their employers paid a weekly sum of money (National Insurance) to the State. In return the workers would get benefits:

unemployment and sickness pay, old age pensions, widows' pensions, death grants and maternity grants.

## Health care

Aneurin Bevan, the Health Minister, wanted to provide a free **National Health Service** for everyone. The 1946 Act made medical and hospital treatment, and treatment by dentists and opticians, free. Clinics were set up to provide care for children and pregnant women.

*Milk was provided free to schoolchildren. Can you think of any reasons why?*

What do you think is happening in this picture?

1. The cartoon on the right was drawn in the 1940s. Which report was the subject of the cartoon?

2. The destination of the bus is CIVILIZATION. Which 'way' must it take to reach its destination?

3. How does the cartoon show that most people liked the ideas in the Beveridge Report?

4. What is the cartoonist saying is the best way forward for Britain?

In the 1980s and 1990s the Conservative government made a number of changes which affected the Welfare State. They set up hospital trusts, introduced charges for optical and dental treatment; and made changes in unemployment and social security benefits.

CLASS ACTIVITY

As a group discuss the following questions:

1. How did the Welfare State affect the lives of ordinary people?

2. What was life like for people before the Welfare State?

3. Why was it such a popular idea after the War?

# The Fifties:
# A great time to be young

Memories may be different from what is known to have happened.

After the hard times of the Depression and the War, life in the 1950s began to seem better. In 1951 the Festival of Britain was held in London. It showed new inventions and designs, and the achievements of Britain.

It became easier to get jobs. People had more money to spend. Young people could buy the new fashions in clothes. They could buy records, and go to cinemas, dance halls and coffee bars. The American word 'teenager' was used to describe this new group of consumers.

American influence was also important in the cinema and pop music. Young people copied film stars like Marilyn Monroe and James Dean.

Elvis Presley and Bill Haley and his Comets were favourite rock and roll stars; also Buddy Holly and Brenda Lee.

The Festival of Britain site on the South Bank of the Thames, in London, and (below) the British 'Comet' jet airliner – the first jet airliner to enter regular commercial service.

Elvis Presley

26

Many families took an annual holiday, usually at the seaside. Holiday camps, such as Butlins, were popular. They provided a chalet to live in, food and entertainment.

In the 1950s, BBC radio programmes like *The Goon Show* and *Hancock's Half Hour* had big audiences.

A new form of entertainment, BBC television, was also becoming popular. In 1950 there were about 3,000 sets in use. Today, almost every household has a television set. A second channel, Independent Television (ITV) began in 1955. BBC 2 began in 1964, and Channel 4 in 1982.

A teenage girl remembers:

We had our first set in 1952. Of course it was a small black and white screen and there was only one channel: BBC. All my aunts, uncles and cousins came round to watch the Cup Final and the Coronation in 1953.

A juke box was a big attraction. By looking at the picture can you explain what it was and how it worked?

## CLASS ACTIVITY

This section suggests that television, teenagers and American films and music were the main features of life in the 1950s. Do people who grew up then agree with this?

To find out, organise a survey called LOOKING BACK.

As a class, draw up a list of questions to ask people who grew up in the 1950s. Compare their answers with what you have read here.

Which memories are similar? Which are different?

How do you explain the differences?

What do your findings tell you about the accuracy of different kinds of historical evidence?

# Immigrants to Britain

People from other countries have settled in Britain for thousands of years. Each group has brought its own culture and language.

In 1930 the British Empire and Commonwealth contained about one quarter of the world's population. Some of these people left their own countries to come and fight on Britain's side in the Second World War (1939-45) (see pages 14–15).

After 1945 there was a shortage of workers so the Government gave Commonwealth citizens the right to come and live here.

In the 1950s there was a rise in the number of **immigrants** – people from other countries coming to live here – from the West Indies

What do you know about the way of life in the West Indies?

What would someone coming from the West Indies for the first time notice was different about Britain?

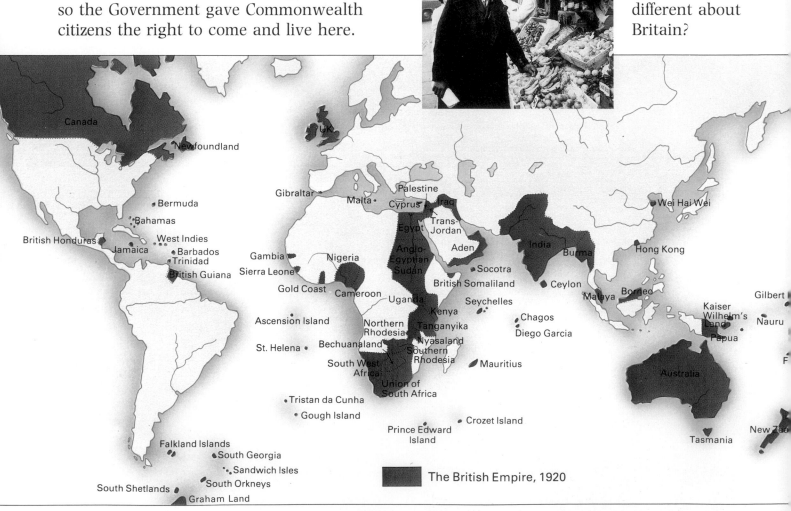

Canada
Newfoundland
UK
Gibraltar
Palestine
Malta
Cyprus
Iraq
Wei Hai Wei
Bermuda
Trans-Jordan
Bahamas
Egypt
British Honduras
West Indies
Aden
India
Hong Kong
Jamaica
Barbados
Trinidad
Gambia
Nigeria
Anglo-Egyptian Sudan
Burma
British Guiana
Sierra Leone
Socotra
Gold Coast
Cameroon
British Somaliland
Ceylon
Borneo
Gilbert
Uganda
Seychelles
Malaya
Kaiser Wilhelm's Land
Nauru
Ascension Island
Kenya
Chagos
Northern Rhodesia
Tanganyika
Diego Garcia
Papua
St. Helena
Bechuanaland
Nyasaland
Southern Rhodesia
South West Africa
Mauritius
Australia
Union of South Africa
Tristan da Cunha
Gough Island
Crozet Island
New Zea
Prince Edward Island
Tasmania
Falkland Islands
South Georgia
Sandwich Isles
South Orkneys
South Shetlands
Graham Land

The British Empire, 1920

This map of the British Empire and Commonwealth in 1920 shows the countries from which many of Britain's immigrants came. Many people also left Britain (emigrated) to live and work abroad.

Immigrant workers played an important part in Britain. Some industries, for example transport and health, could not have provided a good service without them.

The different immigrant styles of music, art and fashion brought variety to the way of life. Many immigrants, and their sons and daughters, became valued members of society.

From the 1960s, fewer workers were needed. Some people called for some immigrants to be sent back to their country of origin. They also wanted less immigration in the future.

In 1962 a law was passed to limit the numbers of immigrants from Commonwealth countries. The law meant that many Commonwealth citizens who had British passports could no longer come to live in Britain. Other laws were also passed to control immigration.

*People of many races enjoying themselves at the Notting Hill Carnival.*

Between 1965 and 1976 laws were passed to protect immigrant people who were already living in Britain. It became illegal to act against people because of their colour, their religion or their race.

This is called **racial discrimination**.

Can you say why racial discrimination is unfair and unjust?

*Children playing together in a school playground.*

CLASS ACTIVITY

In pairs or small groups collect information for a class display on one of the following topics to show how immigrants or their descendants are important in everyday life:

restaurants; sport; shops; hospitals; transport; local factories; music; television and radio; local religious buildings; the local council.

# Changes in the home

We can find out
about the past in
many different ways.

The pictures on these two pages show a living room and a kitchen in the 1950s.

In what ways are the rooms different from the living room and kitchen in your home?

What things are the same?

Can you explain why some things have changed a lot while others have changed very little?

As well as using photographs as a source to tell us about the past, we can also find out in other ways. We can look at things that were in use then: household items – china, for example, or at the clothes that were worn.

We can also talk to people about the past. We can ask them questions and their answers can provide us with historical evidence. This is called a survey.

## CLASS ACTIVITY

Find out what life at home in Britain was like in the 1930s, 1940s and 1950s by asking people living at the time what they remember.

In groups talk about and write down:

What you want to know about.
What questions you might ask to help you find out.

Here are some ideas to help you begin:

1. How was the house heated?

2. How was the cooking and washing done?

3. What was the kitchen like?

4. What electrical goods were used?

5. Was there an indoor toilet and a bathroom?

6. Is your home still there?

7. Has the area changed?

When you have your list of questions, decide which are the most important.

You will need to decide how you will record the answers you receive.

You might need to design a questionnaire where people tick boxes. Or you might want to record interviews on tape or video cassette.

Look at each decade – period of ten years – and say what has changed since then and what has stayed the same.

# Views of the Sixties

Here are four pictures from the 1960s.

Two people were asked to choose pictures showing two of the most important memories of those ten years.

The first two, of The Beatles and England's World Cup victory in 1966, were chosen by someone who was a teenager during that time.

The second pair show what an historian thought were the most important events: President Kennedy's assassination in 1963 and the first man on the moon in 1969.

Look carefully at the pictures to see what they can tell you.

How do these sources show that America had a strong influence on Britain in the 1960s?

How do you know, from the evidence, that the Americans were the first to get a man on the moon?

Moon landing in 1969.

This photograph of President Kennedy's car was taken seconds after the American president was shot.

Ask someone who lived in the 1960s if they remember:

1. exactly what they were doing when they heard the news of President Kennedy's death in 1963.

2. what happened in the final few minutes of England's World Cup victory game in 1966?

What do their answers tell you about how, why and what people remember about events in the past?

This cartoon by Giles was printed in the Daily Express in July 1969.

"All clear, everybody – they've gone."

When finding out about the past you have to remember that people have different ideas and views of what happened.

Think about how the sources in this section might not give a complete picture of life in Britain in the 1960s. How might you get a more complete view?

## CLASS ACTIVITY

In pairs or small groups, find out about one of the following:

• the mini skirt • Carnaby Street •
Concorde (1969) • Telstar (1962)
• BBC 2 television channel (1964) •
comprehensive schools • Open University
• Britain's attempts to join the Common
Market • Beeching Report (1963) •

Put together the findings of all the groups as a classroom display of the 1960s.

# The role of women

Since 1930 the role of women has continued to improve. This is mainly because of the efforts of women themselves. However, events and changes in society have also helped to make life better for them.

Look at pages 20-21.
Write down some of the ways in which the Second World War affected and changed women's lives.

Birth control has meant smaller families and greater freedom for women. Machines to do some of the housework have given women more time to work outside the home.

Patricia Scotland, Britain's first black woman QC (Queen's Counsel). A QC is an important lawyer.

Think of equipment in your home which saves time and effort.

Can you find out when it became common for most homes to have these items?

Today most, but not all, jobs are open to women. Do you know of any women who are doctors, lawyers, police constables, politicians or engineers?

Which jobs or professions are not yet open to women?

Shopping habits have changed. Large chain stores and supermarkets save time as most shopping can be done in one place. They are also open longer hours so people can shop after work.

New technology such as computers and word processors have provided new kinds of work for women.

Betty Boothroyd, speaker of the House of Commons.

This century new laws have given women more rights. In 1928 they were given the right to vote at twenty-one.

Later laws meant that men and women doing the same job had to be paid the same wage. It was made unlawful for anyone to act against a person just because of their gender (that is, whether they are male or female). This is called **sex discrimination**.

Above: Helen Sharman, the first British astronaut, with her Russian colleagues. Right: Rebecca Stephens, the first British woman to climb Mount Everest.

If women do more work outside the home, should men share the work in the home? What do you think?

My husband still expects me to do all the cooking and washing even though I work full time. I don't feel much better off than my mother who was a housewife.

Margaret Thatcher, the first woman British prime minister.

## CLASS ACTIVITY

Get together in small groups and each take one famous name from the following list. Find out why they are famous, and make a display with information and pictures you collect about them.

Amy Johnson, Vera Lynn, Christine Truman, Margot Fonteyn, Agatha Christie, Enid Blyton, Barbara Hepworth, Edith Sitwell, Kathleen Ferrier, Vivien Leigh, Jacqueline Du Pre, Ninette de Valois, Betty Boothroyd, Edith Evans, Sybil Thorndike, Ethel Mary Smyth, Tessa Sanderson.

If you want you could choose someone who is not on this list.

Changes in transport
may not all have been
for the better.

# Britain on the move

After 1930 cheaper cars and plentiful petrol made motoring very popular.

The best-known cars were made by the British company, Morris, and the American firm, Ford. It produced the Ford Eight. Famous Morris cars included the Morris Minor of the 1940s and the Mini of the 1950s.

More road traffic meant more accidents. Better roads and more safety rules were needed. Speed limits were set. Traffic lights were put up.

The Minister of Transport, Mr Hore-Belisha, wanted people to be able to cross busy roads safely. Crossing signs – **Belisha Beacons** – were named after him.

By what other methods do we cross roads more safely today?

Many ways are used to help cut down road accidents. Find out and write about:

1. The **MOT** test

2. The **Green Cross Code**

3. The '**Don't Drink and Drive**' campaign.

What other ways do you know?

The first motorway in Britain (the M1) was opened in the 1950s. Since then others have been built.

Use a road map or atlas to find out and name the motorways in Britain and the cities that they link. Describe the routes they take (north-south; east-west). Which main towns and cities do they pass near?

The Morris Mini

| Year | Number of cars in Britain | Number of people killed by cars | Number of people killed per 1,000 cars |
|------|------|------|------|
| 1930 | 1 million | 7,300 | 7.3 |
| 1939 | 2 million | 6,500 | 3.25 |
| 1951 | 2.4 million | 5,250 | 2.2 |
| 1961 | 6 million | 6,900 | 1.15 |
| 1966 | 9.5 million | 8,000 | 0.85 |
| 1973 | 13.8 million | 7,400 | 0.54 |
| 1977 | 14.2 million | 6,600 | 0.46 |
| 1990 | 22 million | 5,217 | 0.24 |

Cars and their victims, from 1930 to 1990

The railways used to be run by private companies until 1947 when they were taken into public ownership.

Steam trains were gradually replaced by diesel engines and electric locomotives. These were cleaner and cost less to run than steam trains.

In the 1960s, thousands of miles of rail track and many railway stations were closed.

Large lorries now carry most of the goods we need to local shops.

Would it be better if railways or canals carried more goods?

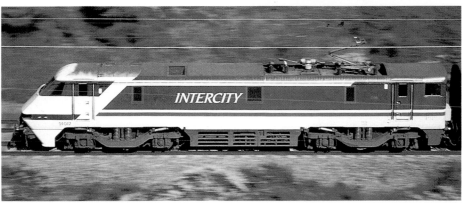

An electric Inter-City express train and above right, the 'Mallard' steam locomotive.

The four photographs on these two pages show different forms of transport. Can you find out in which order of time they each first appeared?

Below, the Concorde jet airliner

Here are some points for and against road transport.

**FOR**
Goods can go directly from one point to another.
Cost is kept down as few people are involved.

**AGAINST**
Vehicles create exhaust fumes and noise.
Heavy lorries damage road surfaces, bridges and houses.
Traffic jams often build up in and near towns.
Can you think of others?

CLASS ACTIVITY

Collect timetables from your local bus and rail stations. Work out and compare the differences for journeys by coach/bus and by train:

1. in times taken

2. in fare prices.

What other differences are there which might make one form of public transport better than another?

# British industry since 1930

The highest unemployment in the 1930s happened in areas where many people worked in one of the 'old' industries.

These were mainly in the north of Britain. The main examples were:

| INDUSTRY | AREA |
|---|---|
| Ship-building | Scotland, Northern Ireland, north-east England |
| Coal-mining | Scotland, northern England, Wales |
| Cotton and woollen textiles | Yorkshire, Lancashire |
| Iron and steel | northern England |

These industries did not modernise their machinery or their ways of making goods. They could not compete with industries in other countries, especially Germany and the United States.

New 'light' industries were based mainly in the Midlands and south-east England. These included Morris Motors at Oxford, and Hoover washing machines and vacuum cleaners. This American company had its main factory in Middlesex

Old advertisements can often show us how people lived. These examples are from the 1930s. What do they tell us about the products and people who bought them? Compare them to present day adverts for biscuits and car tyres.

Other 'new' industries made artificial silk and radios, processed food, or refined petroleum from imported oil. The chemical industry grew as new types of drugs and disinfectants and plastic products appeared.

The new industries needed scientists and technicians rather than strong manual workers. They used electricity as a form of power, so they no longer needed to be near the coalfields. Many new industries were built near London. This was because London was a banking centre. It was also a port from which goods could be sent abroad.

Compare these photographs. What are the main differences between working in a mine and a car factory?

Do sources like this give us a true picture?

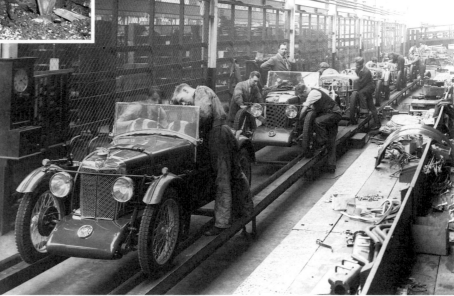

Old and new industries: a coal-mine in Northumberland and the MG car production line at Abingdon, part of Morris Motors, Oxford.

Today many more people work in offices, rather than factories, compared to the 1930s. This is partly because there are up-to-date machines to do the work that people used to do. But it is also because many industries in Britain have closed down or cut back so fewer goods are made. British industries have found it hard to compete with other countries when selling products to consumers.

In the 1980s microcomputers were introduced to make both work and communication more efficient – that means cheaper and quicker.

CLASS ACTIVITY

Make a wall chart listing changes in industry since 1930.

Collect pictures showing people at work in different industries today.

Try to talk to one or two people who have worked in the same job for many years.

What changes have they noticed?

# Scotland, Wales and Northern Ireland

The United Kingdom is made up of Scotland, Wales, Northern Ireland and England. The government and the Houses of Parliament are in London. MPs (see page 42) from all four countries talk about important matters and make and pass laws.

## SCOTLAND

Most people live in the central area between Glasgow and Edinburgh.

Since 1930 coal-mining, ship-building and engineering have declined (see pages 38-9).

After 1970 oil from the North Sea brought wealth to the Aberdeen area. At the same time the fishing industry became less important.

The Scottish Nationalist Party wants Scotland to have its own government in Edinburgh.

*Winter holidays in the Scottish Highlands.*

## WALES

Many old industries have closed down, including iron and steel and coal-mining.

Some new factories have been built but many Welsh people have moved to England to find work.

Welsh culture remains strong. A festival of literature and music (The Eisteddfod) is held each year. The Welsh language is widely spoken and taught in schools.

The Nationalist Party in Wales is called Plaid Cymru.

# NORTHERN IRELAND

In 1921 most of Ireland became independent from the United Kingdom and is now called the Irish Republic. Its people are mainly Roman Catholic.

Ulster (Northern Ireland) stayed part of Britain. Most people there are Protestants but a large number are Catholics.

Some people, including many Catholics, wanted Ireland to be united as one country. They want Northern Ireland to become part of Eire. Others, for example many Protestants, are against this.

Organised terrorist groups fight to try and get their own way. These include the Irish Republican Army (IRA) and the Ulster Defence Association (UDA).

In 1969 British troops were sent to Ulster to try to keep the peace. However, the troubles continue and bomb attacks take place in both Northern Ireland and on mainland Britain.

Ship-building in Northern Ireland has declined causing many people to be out of work. In 1986-87 the government spent £1,700 million to build up new industries. Some businesses are now booming there.

Ulster Protestants in procession.

What similar changes have taken place in these three countries?

What different kinds of changes can you find?

**Clues**: jobs; political ideas; violence and unrest.

Learning to read in a Welsh school.

---

## CLASS ACTIVITY

In groups, or as a class, find out about the culture and customs of one of the four nations of the United Kingdom.

What are their flags, national emblems, saints, costumes, music, folk songs and dances?

You could organise a 'Four Nations' morning and show other groups or classes what you have found.

# How Britain is governed

*Different features of a situation are linked to each other.*

Britain has a **monarch** (king or queen) and a **Parliamentary government**.

The present monarch is Queen Elizabeth II who began her reign in 1952. She is the Head of State in Britain, and Head of the Church of England. She is also Head of the Commonwealth.

There are two 'houses' of Parliament. The House of Commons has elected members of Parliament (MPs). The members of the House of Lords are unelected.

In a General Election people over the age of 18 (except those in prison, in mental hospital or the House of Lords) can vote for an MP to represent them in the House of Commons. The party with most members in the Commons can form a government. Choosing a government by people voting is called **democracy**.

The Conservative Party won most seats in the 1992 General Election and formed the government. The main opposition parties are Labour and the Liberal Democrats. For most of the second half of the twentieth century the Conservative party has governed Britain.

The State Opening of Parliament takes place each year. It is the one time when the monarch, the members of the House of Lords and the House of Commons meet together.

Can you identify these people in the picture? What do you notice about their positions?

*The State Opening of Parliament.*

The Mace-bearer, Black Rod and the Speaker of the House of Commons lead Members of Parliament in procession to the House of Lords.

At this ceremony members of the House of Commons demand entry to the House of Lords to hear the monarch speak about the plans of the government.

What does this ceremony tell us about the role of the monarch, the Lords and the Commons?

The **European Economic Community** (EEC) was set up by the Treaty of Rome in 1957. Six nations signed the Treaty. Britain joined in 1973. By 1990 there were twelve member countries. They have agreed to buy and sell goods (trade) more freely with each other.

Identify each of the flags and link them with the correct EEC member states.

Find these countries on a map of Europe. Which European countries are not members of the European Community?

CLASS ACTIVITY

Design a flag or set of stamps which you think best shows the nature of the European Community.

You can use paper and paint or pens; sewing silks, cotton and material; or computer graphics.

In what ways might the Channel Tunnel between Britain and France improve trade and other links between the countries of the European Community?

A French express train emerges from the Channel Tunnel in England.

# World problems: World solutions

Some of the problems which affect Britain are also world problems, which are caused by many countries. They can only be solved by countries working together.

## Our environment

The way we live and work causes the pollution of our environment. The use of fossil fuels (coal, oil and gas) for energy and the growth of road transport have increased the amount of sulphur dioxide in the air. This can cause **acid rain** which poisons oceans, trees and lakes.

The oceans are also poisoned with waste products from the nuclear and oil industries and the chemicals used in farming. Chemicals escaping into the atmosphere are also breaking down the **ozone layer**.

The richest nations use up most of the earth's natural resources. These countries also produce most waste and cause most environmental pollution.

Nuclear power stations produce 18 per cent of Britain's energy. The first in Britain (Windscale) was opened in Cumbria in 1956. It was later renamed Sellafield.

The waste from nuclear power stations is **radioactive** and therefore dangerous. People argue about whether there are any safe ways to store this. There are also dangers of nuclear explosions and radiation leaks.

In 1986 the nuclear power station at Chernobyl in Russia exploded. How does this show that problems caused by one country can have worldwide consequences?

Chernobyl Nuclear Power Station in Russia, 1986.

A 'Lollipop Lady' in London wearing an anti-pollution mask.

## Food and health

The number of people in the world has more than doubled since 1950. The increase has been greatest in parts of Asia, Africa and South America.

Food production has not kept up with growing demand. This is especially true in parts of Africa where droughts can bring famine and disaster.

Many countries and organisations such as the United Nations are trying to help with food and seed as well as advice on better methods of farming.

Starving children in Africa and (above) the destruction of tropical forests in South America.

Better diets and medical care mean that people in Britain are living longer. Since the 1930s, many childhood illnesses have been prevented by vaccination, and many other diseases have been cured.

However, in poorer parts of the world, lack of good food, water and medicine mean that people still die of illnesses which could be cured. A new disease called AIDS is now spreading through many rich and poor countries.

CLASS ACTIVITY

Talk about some of the problems in Britain which are also world problems.

Can you suggest ways in which world leaders might try to solve them?

Talk about the ways in which you or your class, in your everyday lives, might help to solve them.

Perhaps you could organise a campaign or project to safeguard the environment?

# The story of my life by Susan

Susan was born on 1 January 1930.

This is her time line of the twenty most important events in her life:

1930 I was born.

1939 War began against Germany. I was evacuated to the countryside.

1945 Peace at last! Dad came home from the army.

1946 I started work at the shoe factory.

1951 My 21st birthday. I voted for the first time in the General Election. We had our first television.

1953 Coronation Year. I married Jim that August.

WAY IN

BALLOT BOX 151

1954 The twins, Jane and David, were born on 3 July.

1959 We moved to London where Jim found a new job on a newspaper. A really hot summer.

1963 Our first holiday abroad. We flew to Majorca.

1970 David left school and went to work in Norwich. What a change!

1972 Mum died from a heart attack. A hard time for us all. Jim's job wasn't going well and Jane had 'A' levels. Still she got to university.

1973 Jim changed jobs but we stayed put. Everything got so expensive because of an oil shortage. There was some trouble in the Middle East.

1975 Jane got her English degree and began teacher training.

1976 David married Hilary at Lincoln.

1977 I met the Queen. It was her Silver Jubilee and she visited the canteen where I worked.

1978 I am a grandmother for the first time! Our Silver Wedding.

1981 Dad died.

1982 Jane married Michael. Both teachers so they had very little to begin with.

1989 Jim retired. We moved to Margate near Jane and Michael who now have two children.

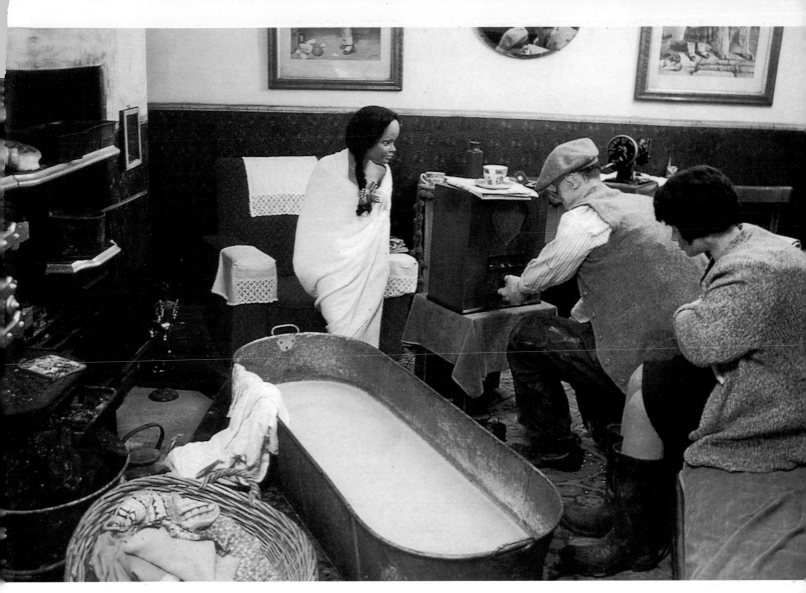

*The day war broke out, 1939. We were all gathered round the wireless. I was just about to get into the tin bath in front of the fire. I had to be clean for the evacuation journey the next day.*

The time line on the opposite page is mostly about Susan's family life.

What national events does she remember?

What changes affected Susan's way of life?

If you were putting together Susan's life story, how useful would the time line be?

What other evidence would you use?

## CLASS ACTIVITY

Make your own time line. Begin with your birth. Put all the events of your family life above the time line.

In groups, add important national and international events below the time line.

Look at the completed chart. Did any national events affect or change your family life?

A grandmother living in happy retirement in Margate. How old is Susan today?

47

# Index